Stephen
and the
Family Nose

a novel by
Catherine Storr

Chapter 1

When Stephen was six he decided to run away from home.

When Stephen was seven he began to save his pocket money and his birthday money for the time when he would go.

When Stephen was eight,
he ran away.

Why did he run?

It wasn't because he
had a cruel Mum and Dad.
In fact, they were nice and
he liked them a lot.

It wasn't because he
was bullied at school.
In fact, he got on well
at school and he had
a lot of friends.

It wasn't because he had fights with his
sister. She was four years younger than
him, and she was all right ...

...most of the time.

The trouble was his grandma and grandpa and his uncles and aunts. Especially his aunts.

Whenever they saw him, one of them would make a remark about what he looked like.

They didn't just say, "He has curly hair," or "He has a blobby nose," or "He has grey eyes." Instead they said things like:

That's the family nose, it's exactly like Grandpa's.

His Aunt Janet gave him those grey eyes.

Stephen's got a good ear, perhaps he's going to be musical like his Uncle James.

When he first heard this, Stephen had thought that "a good ear" meant what shape his ears were, but when he got older he realized that it was a way of saying that he could tell one tune from another.

Everything about Stephen seemed to have belonged to someone else in the family first.

His relations had been talking like this ever since he'd been born.

While he was still a baby, Stephen hadn't minded. But when he grew older, he hated it. He began to feel as if he wasn't a real person at all, but just a lot of bits of the family put together.

He wanted to shout at them, "I'm not *just like* any of you. I'm me! I'll run away to somewhere where no one knows me or my family. Then no one will say I'm like *anyone*."

Chapter 2

Stephen decided to run away when the weather was warm, in case he had to sleep out of doors. One Saturday that summer, he put some spare clothes and all the money from his moneybox into his backpack.

Then he had to wait until his mother had gone out shopping before he could escape out of the house. He did not want her to ask where he was going.

He decided to take the bus to
Longbourn Station, near to where his
Aunt Janet lived. He had made this
journey by himself before, but this time he
meant to catch a train from the station to
somewhere far away.

When Stephen got out of the bus he went into the station. He saw that there was no one in the ticket office. He looked through the little window and saw a small room with the machine that printed tickets, and racks of leaflets on the walls.

An open door opposite him led to a more comfortable-looking room where he saw a chair with cushions. On a table were a mug, a television, a newspaper and a microwave which was humming to itself.

Stephen knocked on the little window of the booking office. After a minute or two, a man came through the door and said, "Yes?"

"Where does the next train go to?" Stephen asked.

The man rattled off a list of names too quickly for Stephen to catch most of them. But the list ended with one he knew. Sealands. He had been there once. He remembered a long stony beach and a smell of seaweed. Huge grey waves, seagulls screaming overhead. A good place to run away to.

Stephen said, "A ticket to Sealands, please."

"Single or return?" the man asked.

"Single." You didn't buy a return ticket if you were running away, thought Stephen.

"Seven pounds eighty," the man said.

This was terrible. Stephen hadn't got anything like as much as seven pounds eighty. He said, "I go half price."

"I can see that. It's still seven pounds eighty," the man said.

"I'll have to think about it," Stephen said. This was what his mum always said when she found that something she wanted to buy would cost more money than she had.

The man was just beginning to say, "Take your time," when Stephen interrupted him.

He said, "There's a funny smell."

"Didn't you wash this morning?" the man said, nastily.

"It's something burning," Stephen said.

"Think you're being funny?" the man said.

Then suddenly he realized what Stephen had said. He turned round and ran back into his room behind the ticket office.

The microwave was almost hidden in a cloud of smoke. Stephen was almost sure he saw flames through the smoke.

The man grabbed a blue fire extinguisher and in a moment the microwave was covered with powder.

What was left was a horrible sticky mess, but there was no more smoke.

The man put down the extinguisher and sat down heavily on the chair. "That's my dinner gone," he said.

"There was nearly a fire," Stephen said.

"Too right. And then what would I have told the Inspector? Lucky for me you smelled it," the man said.

"I have a very good nose," Stephen said. As he said it, he remembered what the family had said about his nose.

They had said that it was Grandpa's nose, and that had made Stephen feel as if he had no right to it. But now that he had saved the ticket office and possibly the whole station from being burned down, he felt better about his nose. Wherever it had come from, it was he, Stephen, who had used it to smell burning.

"Want that ticket? I'll pay," the man said.

"No, thank you. I've changed my mind," Stephen said, and he walked out of the station.

Chapter 3

Just outside, he saw his Uncle Frisby with the dog. Uncle Frisby said, "Hi!"

"Hi!" said Stephen.

"Coming to see us? Your Aunt Janet's been baking this morning," Uncle Frisby said.

As soon as he had spoken, Stephen could almost smell Aunt Janet's baking. She always baked on Saturday mornings, and she almost always made a special sort of gingerbread that was unbelievably delicious.

Stephen's nose remembered that smell. It made his mouth water. He *had* to say that he would go back with his Uncle Frisby.

When they got to the house, Aunt Janet was just taking a tray out of the oven. She said, "Stephen? Would you rather have a gingerbread rabbit or a gingerbread man or a gingerbread elephant? Only I'm afraid its trunk has gone a bit funny."

Stephen chose the elephant with the funny trunk. He had to wait a little until the gingerbread was cool enough to eat.

"Did you find it?" Uncle Frisby asked Aunt Janet.

"No. And I've looked everywhere. There's been a magpie around the house this morning. I think it must have come into the kitchen while I was upstairs and stolen it," Aunt Janet said.

Uncle Frisby said, "Nonsense, birds don't do that sort of thing!"

But Aunt Janet said, "Yes they do, I've heard a whole opera about a magpie stealing jewellery."

"What has the magpie stolen?"
Stephen asked.

"My best ring. I took it off when I was
baking, and now I can't find it," Aunt
Janet said.

Stephen ate a bit of the elephant. It
was delicious.

He said, "Shall I look for your ring,
Aunt Janet?"

"You can if you like. But you won't find it. I told you, I've looked everywhere, and it's gone for good," his aunt said.

Stephen finished the elephant. He looked hungrily at the gingerbread man, but he did not like to ask for it. So he wandered round the kitchen, looking in all the places where he thought the ring might be.

He looked behind jars...

under shelves...

between pots of jam and marmalade...

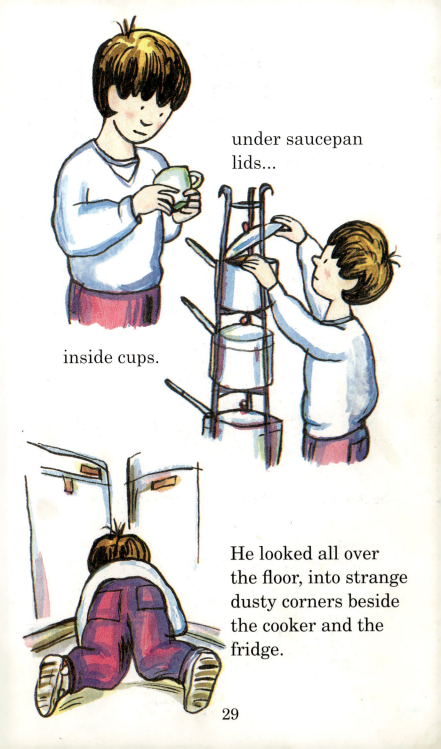

under saucepan
lids...

inside cups.

He looked all over
the floor, into strange
dusty corners beside
the cooker and the
fridge.

"I told you, I've looked everywhere," Aunt Janet said, rather crossly.

But just at that moment, Stephen saw something. It was a sparkle, a flash of light.

The sun had come out from behind a cloud and sent a ray through the kitchen window, on to something that shone back like a star.

On one of the cup hooks on the kitchen dresser, was hanging ... not a cup, but a ring. A ring with a bright stone, which reflected back the sun's ray with a rainbow of its own.

"Stephen! You clever boy! To think that I missed seeing my own ring! You must have very good eyes! Much better than mine," Aunt Janet said, handing him the gingerbread man without being asked.

"Magpies, indeed," Uncle Frisby said, walking out of the kitchen.

Stephen bit into the gingerbread man. He tasted even better than the elephant. Stephen thought, "Aunt Janet says my eyes are better than hers. So they are really my very own eyes." He felt terribly pleased.

"You didn't walk all the way here, did you? Was there anything special you came for?" Aunt Janet asked.

Stephen did not want to tell her that he had really set out to run away. He said, "I just came to see you. Mum asked me to bring you her love."

"That was very nice of her. If you're not in a hurry to get back home, Stephen, I wonder if you'd drop in at Uncle James' house, just along the road? Would you tell him and Aunt Sara that I'm expecting them to tea tomorrow? When they're both practising their music they often don't answer the telephone, and I haven't got time this morning to go round there myself."

Stephen said, "Of course I will!" Then he picked up his backpack and started off along the road.

Chapter 4

Some time before he arrived at Uncle
James' house, Stephen could hear music
coming through the open windows. But it
didn't sound like Uncle James' violin or
Aunt Sara's piano. It sounded more like
music on the radio or television.

When Aunt Sara opened the door, she said, in a great hurry, "Come in quickly, we're trying to win a quiz." Which didn't make sense to Stephen, until he was in the living room and he saw what she meant.

The television was on, and a man was saying, "The next piece of music I'm going to play is for full orchestra. Can anyone name it?" Then the orchestra appeared on the screen, playing a marching sort of music with a lot of trumpets and drums.

"I know what that is – Handel," Uncle James said, and he wrote something down on a sheet of paper he had on the table in front of him.

"How many is that?" Aunt Sara asked.

"That's nineteen. One more," said Uncle James, just as the man on the TV screen was saying, "Now, here's something for our younger viewers."

The picture on the screen changed to show a pop group with three guitars and a drummer, playing a piece Stephen had heard before.

"Know what that is?" Aunt Sara asked Uncle James.

"Of course I don't. I don't listen to that sort of music, if you can call it music," said Uncle James, in a very bad temper.

"We've got all the others. It'll be very annoying if we have to send in the form with one answer missing," Aunt Sara said.

"It isn't worth the postage stamp unless we've got the lot," Uncle James said.

"We've got nineteen. And you said it was very hard," Aunt Sara argued.

Stephen said,

I know that last tune ...

... but Uncle James interrupted him. "I don't know why we do these stupid competitions. Pure waste of time."

Stephen said ...

I know ...

... and this time Aunt Sara
said, "What do you know?"

I know that last tune.
I've heard it on the telly!

"So what is it called?" Aunt Sara asked.

"It's called *Rings On My Fingers*. Everyone was playing it last year," Stephen said.

"*RINGS ON MY FINGERS*? Stupid name," said Uncle James, but he was writing it down on his paper, and he seemed to have stopped being angry.

"Thank you, Stephen. What a clever boy you are!" Aunt Sara said.

"Tell you what. I've got to go to the post office with this, why don't I take you back home in the car?" Uncle James said.

Stephen did not like to say, "No thanks, I'm running away." So five minutes later he found himself in the car with Uncle James, now in a very good temper, humming to himself as he drove. He posted his answer form in the post office and then let Stephen out at the gate of his home.

Chapter 5

"Where have you been all the morning?" Stephen's mum asked as he came into the kitchen.

"I went to see Aunt Janet. And she asked me to go round to Uncle James. And then Uncle James brought me home in his car."

"That was kind of him," Stephen's mum said.

"I helped him finish the answers to a quiz on the telly."

"Clever boy. But why did you go over to see Aunt Janet?"

"She gave me a gingerbread elephant," Stephen said.

"I hope it won't have spoiled your appetite for dinner. Go and wash your hands," Stephen's mum said.

Stephen looked at himself in the mirror over the washbasin. He looked just the same as always. Aunt Janet's eyes. Grandpa's nose. Uncle James' ears. But today he didn't feel the same about them.

His nose might be like Grandpa's but it was Stephen who had smelled the burning microwave in the station.

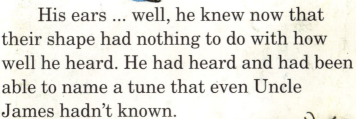

His eyes might be like Aunt Janet's but it was Stephen who had used them to find the ring.

His ears ... well, he knew now that their shape had nothing to do with how well he heard. He had heard and had been able to name a tune that even Uncle James hadn't known.

"*My* nose. *My* eyes. *My* ears. I'm not just bits of other people stuck together. I can do things they can't. I'm myself, I'm Stephen. I'm like the family, but I'm different too. I'm special," Stephen said to his reflection in the mirror. "You're the only one who is really exactly like me," Stephen said to it. His reflection looked back at Stephen …

… and smiled.